SEA MONSTERS

ENDURING MYSTERIES

KEN KARST

Published by
CREATIVE EDUCATION and CREATIVE PAPERBACKS

P.O. Box 227, Mankato, Minnesota 56002
Creative Education and Creative Paperbacks are imprints of The Creative Company
www.thecreativecompany.us

Design by Danny Nanos of Gilbert & Nanos
Production by Joe Kahnke
Art direction by Rita Marshall
Printed in China

Photographs by Alamy (Amanda Cotton, dieKleinert, Nature Picture Library, Jeff Rotman, Stocktrek Images, Inc.),
Canadian Postage Stamps (Ralph Tibbles, Allan Cormack, Deborah Drew-Brook), Creative Commons Wikimedia
(William Frederick Mitchell, Reinhold Möller, Carole Raddato/Flickr, Pavel Riha), Getty Images (Dorling Kindersley,
John Lund/Blend Images, Portland Press Herald, Universal History Archive/Universal Images Group), iStockphoto
(HadelProductions, leoaleks, MR1805, Vaara), Metropolitan Museum of Art (Gift of Ariel Herrmann, in memory of
Brian T. Aitken, 2009), Minden Pictures (Lex van Groningen/Buiten-beeld), Shutterstock (3DMI, best works, cieniu1,
Mike H, Herschel Hoffmeyer, Jannarong, Melkor3D, Konstantin Novikov, OSORIOartist, Sergei Proshchenko, Sofia
Santos, S.Bachstroem, shaineast, Jeff Stamer)

Library of Congress Cataloging-in-Publication Data

Names: Karst, Ken, author.
Title: Sea monsters / Ken Karst.
Series: Enduring mysteries.
Includes bibliographical references and index.
Summary: An investigative approach to the curious phenomena and mysterious circumstances
surrounding sea monsters, from mythological tales to reported sightings to hard facts.

Identifiers: LCCN 2017060034
ISBN 978-1-64026-008-5 (hardcover) / ISBN 978-1-62832-559-1 (pbk) / ISBN 978-1-64000-033-9 (eBook)
Subjects: LCSH: Sea monsters—Juvenile literature.
Classification: LCC GR910.K37 2018 / DDC 001.944—dc23

CCSS: RI.5.1, 2, 3, 6, 8; RH.6–8.4, 5, 6, 7, 8

First Edition HC   9 8 7 6 5 4 3 2 1
First Edition PBK   9 8 7 6 5 4 3 2 1

CREATIVE EDUCATION • CREATIVE PAPERBACKS

Table of Contents

A submarine hums steadily through the deep, blue sea. Suddenly, a large creature overtakes it, followed by several others. The creature jams its enormous, horned beak into the propeller. The sub stops moving, jarring the crew members inside. The crew will have to fight the creature on the surface, the captain announces. They grab axes and a harpoon and climb the ladder to the top hatch. The creature slides one of its suckered arms through the opening. It plucks a sailor out of the ship. The crew is able to slice off many of the monster's tentacles. But the creature shoots a black liquid at them and escapes. The remaining creatures swarm the deck, and the battle continues until "the monsters, vanquished and mutilated, left us at last, and disappeared under the waves." This scene is from Jules Verne's *Twenty Thousand Leagues under the Sea*. That literary work is fictional, of course. But the cuttlefish Verne described have proven to be sea monsters that, like many others, travel freely between the distant past, the human imagination, and the real sea.

CAUTION: MONSTERS BELOW!

The brave Odysseus, hero of Greek **mythology**, saw members of his crew dashed to death on rocks by a sea monster with six heads on long necks. The biblical character of Jonah spent three days and three nights in the belly of a whale before it vomited him to safety on a beach. Captain Ahab, in Herman Melville's *Moby-Dick*, devoted his career to chasing a great white whale. In the end, the whale dragged Ahab down into the sea with him. Beachgoers and fishermen on Long Island in the early 1970s were terrorized by an enormous shark. It was the mechanical star of the movie *Jaws*, adapted from Peter Benchley's novel. And of course there was Godzilla, the massive, dinosaur-like creature, lifted from the deep by nuclear radiation to become a legendary destructive force.

Squid. Whales. Sharks. Godzilla and other dinosaur-like reptiles. Man-eaters of all kinds. Throughout history, the mysteries of the sea and peoples' imaginations have combined to produce a variety of menacing

monsters. Some were real. Some were merely characters in myths, books, and films. Some were a combination of both. In many cases, terrifying sea monsters came about as people tried to describe very real and scary things they had never seen before. Imagine the reaction of the first person to see a seahorse: "So tiny, but there must be big ones around!" they probably thought. Later reports of these tiny, delicate creatures may have transformed them into huge sea creatures with long snouts and spiny tails. Such stories have been a way to remind people to respect and fear the sea—a seemingly bottomless, dark home to unknown things and creatures. In some ways, it's a wonder people have continued sailing, fishing, and swimming at all.

"Undoubtedly, seafaring folk did witness giant creatures in the seas and oceans of the world, and many were hitherto unknown species," writes researcher Paul Harrison in his book, *Sea Serpents and Lake Monsters of the British Isles*. "Those who encountered the whale for the first time could

Despite all the advances in science and technology, people have explored just 5 percent of Earth's oceans to date.

Ancient civilizations left behind many artifacts and legends depicting sea monsters—which could have been long-ago species of real animals.

be forgiven for misinterpreting it as a nemesis of evil, surfacing from the deep to wreak carnage and devastation upon civilization as we know it."

Water covers more than two-thirds of Earth's surface. But humans have explored only 5 percent of the world's seas. "We know more about the moon than the deep sea," says Portuguese marine biologist Rui Rosa. No wonder, then, that sea monsters continue to trigger our imaginations. It's also no wonder that new sea creatures are still being discovered. They turn up in fishing nets, get caught in boat propellers, and wash up on beaches. Sometimes they're photographed or videotaped by scientists in **submersibles** that can travel deeper than ever before. And imaginary ones are always turning up in movies and video games.

There's no way to know the oldest sea monster story. Cave paintings going back nearly 12,000 years to the last ice age show strange sea creatures. Some Babylonian writings from 7,000 years ago mention a fishlike god with feet that came from the Red Sea and taught people how to write. (It also taught them how to grow crops and do math.) Written stories of sea monsters followed. A few thousand years later, Hindu scripture in India presented the story of Ananta Shesha, a sort of endless serpent with anywhere from 100 to 1,000 heads. Its most important role was to hold up the earth. But it also had the power to stir up the sea, making waves and bringing gods and goods from the sea. Hindus also believed in a whale-sized, rainbow-colored fish that ate the wise teacher, Buddha. Buddha was later

10

released by fishermen. The fish was killed and reportedly provided food for a year.

The Egyptian god Apep was a giant serpent that encircled Earth. Apep tried to stop the sun god, Ra, from completing his journey across the sky each day. Apep lurked in the sea near the horizon. Their conflict was represented in each day's fiery sunset. Apep was also blamed for solar eclipses and storms that brought cool conditions. Obviously, Apep has never won his battle with Ra. But he attempts it every day.

In Mesopotamia, the ancient heart of what is now the Middle East, a similar serpentine sea monster emerged. Its name was Labbu. Its body was 300 miles (483 km) long. It had wings. Labbu had a nasty habit of crawling ashore and eating people. A warrior god slayed Labbu.

The Greek poet Homer wrote his *Odyssey* around 700 B.C. In it, Odysseus encounters many dangers on his sailing voyage back to Greece. He has to slip his ship between Scylla, the six-headed monster, and Charybdis, the whirlpool. Scylla's role, in the words of the goddess Circe, is "to plague mankind." Scylla is known for eating one sailor with each of her heads. As Odysseus and his men focus on avoiding the whirlpool, she does just that, grabbing and devouring six of his strongest crew members. But Odysseus gets through the passage.

Gonggong was a Chinese serpent-like figure. He was a redhead, which probably added to his otherworldliness in China, where most people have black hair. Gonggong brought floods and other catastrophes to Earth. His stories emerged about 200 B.C. Like Labbu, Gonggong was destroyed by the gods.

In North America, where early peoples had no knowledge of European or Asian myths, many American Indian tribes acknowledged a being called Unktehi. Unktehi lived in rivers. It was sometimes represented as a horned serpent with the power to unleash floods. The Ojibwe had a lynx- or panther-like water god called Mishipeshu. Mishipeshu was the guardian of the copper mines on Michipicoten Island in eastern Lake Superior. He was credited with killing four copper thieves. He was also believed to be responsible for storms that sometimes sank ships carrying copper. Mishipeshu's image, featuring a menacing stretch of raised fur along his back, was painted on a rock face in Lake Superior Provincial Park. Historians think it was painted sometime in the 17th or 18th century.

There are many more sea monster examples around the globe. The story of Scotland's Loch Ness Monster goes back to the sixth century B.C. The kraken, a tenacious, tentacled attacker, was first described in Norway in 1523. Mermaids and mermen—creatures with human torsos and heads but

scaly fish tails instead of legs—are well known in many cultures. Explorers Christopher Columbus and Henry Hudson both claimed to have seen them.

It's easy to understand why people thought they saw sea monsters. Water is dark. It can hide things. It can also reflect the sun and blind the observer. Waves or flotsam can look like swimming animals. People in the modern world almost always look to scientific explanations for such things. But not long ago, humans were much more willing to regard what couldn't be seen as an extension of what could.

Contemporary author and "investigator of strange creatures" Linda Godfrey writes that stories of sea monsters are "both universal and timeless." To John Steinbeck, one of the great American writers of the 20th century, sea monsters were the residents of the deep sea as well as the deep human mind. "Men really need sea-monsters in their personal ocean," Steinbeck wrote in *The Log from the Sea of Cortez*. "An ocean without its unnamed monsters would be like a completely dreamless sleep."

How to Bag a Sea Monster

History shows it's not easy to find sea monsters. But with some research, good equipment, and a lot of patience, you can improve your chances of seeing one. Even better, you might catch one or prove a legendary monster really exists. First, check local historical accounts and interview anglers, boaters, campers, and local residents. Study maps that show both the shoreline and the depths of the water you'll be searching. Get to know the local vegetation and **terrain**; you don't want to mistake some tree stumps for a serpent. A boat is helpful. So is **scuba** gear. But more important are powerful binoculars, a camera, and a video recording device. At the site, stay calm and organized. You don't want to accidentally drop your camera in the water when a monster emerges. Make regular notes on weather and temperature conditions. A smartphone can double as a notebook and a locator. A tape measure and a fishing net would be useful if you actually get your hands on a monster—provided it's not bigger than your boat. Finally, bring sunscreen and extra food and drinking water. You could be out there for a while—just like the sea monster has been!

MODELS FOR
SEA MONSTERS

Human beings have always wanted explanations. Where does thunder come from? Why are stars arranged the way they are? What makes storms at sea? What calms the water? Is that babbling brook really talking to me?

Long ago, explanations usually came in the form of myths. Many of these stories involved gods. Thunder was typically created by the most powerful god. The stars were put in place by gods to honor someone or to make up for a mistake. Storms at sea were created—and ended—by a mighty water god. And if the brook was speaking, you had better listen. It was probably a god who wanted your attention.

Sea monsters have long been described as godlike. They might have special powers. But some are based on animals that truly exist. Centuries ago, Scandinavian sailors were always on the lookout for a particular water monster. In 1555, Olaus Magnus, the Catholic archbishop of Sweden, described some "horrible" fish that looked like uprooted trees. They had enormous, fiery eyes and beards. They could "drown easily many great ships provided with many strong mariners [sailors]," Magnus wrote. Indeed, an illustration in Magnus's book shows an enormous serpentine creature crushing a sailing ship.

Two centuries later, Erik Ludvigsen Pontoppidan, bishop of Bergen, Norway, heard of a similar monster from fishermen. In a book on the natural history of Norway, Pontoppidan called the monster the kraken. The name comes from a Norwegian word for an uprooted tree. Pontoppidan described it as the largest sea monster in the world. It had many tentacles. And yes, its size was

mind-boggling. Its upper half, Pontoppidan wrote, was one and a half miles (2.4 km) around. It was surrounded by "something that floats and fluctuates like seaweed," he added. Seen from afar, floating on the surface, the creature could easily be mistaken for an island or several islands. No one had ever seen the entire creature, Pontoppidan noted.

Pontoppidan said the kraken threatened ships just by moving. Attracted by the fish that followed the kraken, fishermen who lingered above the creature could be knocked from their boats as it rose up, making huge waves. It often generated an enormous whirlpool when it sank. The English poet Alfred, Lord Tennyson described such a calamity in his 1830 poem "The Kraken."

In later stories, the kraken became smaller but more aggressive. Drawings showed it tossing ships into the air with its tentacles. Then, in the mid-1800s, strange, tentacled creatures started turning up on rocky shores. They looked as though they could have been kraken. But these were giant squid. People had seen them moving quickly through the water before, but they had never been able to inspect one, especially out of the water. Now they could see that it had eight arms with suction cups and two other, much longer tentacles. The giant squid weren't as big as the legendary kraken, but they were still huge and strange.

The giant squid soon replaced the kraken in the halls of monster-hood. The giant squid was a known creature, not a myth. But it was barely known. No live giant squid has ever been captured (without being immediately released or escaping). They seem to prefer to swim at depths from 984 to 3,281 feet (300–1,000 m). Even researchers in submersibles rarely see them. No giant squid was caught on video underwater until 2012.

Although sperm whales feed on giant squid, the squid often leave the whales with suction marks and scars.

A giant squid can change color instantly to match its surroundings. With their instinct for hiding, they are not considered aggressive creatures. Giant squid have the largest eyes of any known animal—11 inches (27.9 cm) across. We don't see them much, but maybe they can see us quite well!

Scientists commonly study parts of giant squid found in the bellies of sperm whales, the only animals known to prey on them. The size of giant squid varies from report to report, partly because their bodies change so much in open, dry air. The largest giant squid on record measured 43 feet (13.1 m) in length. The heaviest weighed about one ton (0.9 t).

The octopus is another living creature strange enough to qualify as a sea monster. Octopuses have three hearts. Unlike most animals, their blood is not iron-based and red. It's copper-based, so it's blue. If octopuses ate peanut butter, they'd be able to twist open the jar with their tentacles, just as they use them to open clams and snails. Like giant squid, they can also match their surroundings, changing color and texture instantly. They can make themselves look like rocks, plants, or algae.

Serpents were a popular type of sea monster for many centuries. Then along came the oarfish—another real sea creature! The oarfish does not get big enough to encircle Earth. But it is the longest bony fish in the world. It can grow to more than 50 feet (15.2 m). A comblike red fin runs the length of its back. On its head, the thin spikes elongate into something resembling a showy feather.

The oarfish was first discovered in the mid-1700s, but it is rarely spotted in the wild. It is not aggressive toward people. The oarfish is not a good swimmer and tends to linger at depths of about 3,000 feet (914 m). It earned its sea-monster status on the rare occasions it ventured into shallower waters.

Two other notable fish swimming in Earth's waters today have existed long enough to qualify as sea monsters. The lake sturgeon, which lives in freshwater lakes and rivers in eastern North America, looks the same today as it did 165 million years ago. Dinosaurs would recognize it! The lake sturgeon is covered in bony plates rather than scaly skin. It's slow-growing but successful. Sturgeon can reach nearly 8 feet (2.4 m) in length and weigh 200 pounds (90.7 kg). Females can live 150 years.

In the sea, the coelacanth (*SEEL-uh-kanth*) was thought to have disappeared 65 million years ago. Fossils were found in the 1800s, but no living example was seen until 1938. More coelacanths have been found and seen in the Indian Ocean since then. Coelacanths can be 6.5 feet (2 m) long and weigh nearly 200 pounds (90.7 kg). That's getting into monster territory. They live in caves deep below the surface and emerge to feed at night. These

Monstrous-looking oarfish (left) and coelacanths (above) might seem scary, but you'll probably never see one of these bottom-dwellers.

23

are good ways to remain hidden.

Manatees might be regarded as sea monsters simply because of their size. They can be 13 feet (4 m) long and weigh about 1,200 pounds (544 kg). But they are gentle mammals. Female manatees often hold their young in their flippers, much like humans cradle babies. Manatees sleep half the day and eat only plants. They like to bob and drift in warm, shallow waters. As a result, they sometimes cross paths with people. Manatees are often injured by boats or from consuming inedible trash. They are considered threatened in the United States.

Manatees, also known as sea cows, are gentle marine animals, but fangtooth fish (opposite) are another story.

Mirror-Breakers Mermaids are the only sea creatures known to check themselves out in mirrors. That might be because so many other creatures are so terrifyingly ugly. The most fearsome might be the Vampire squid. Its scientific name, _Vampyroteuthis infernalis_, translates as "vampire squid from hell." This squid appears to have a red cape that conceals a set of eight arms lined with soft spikes. The anglerfish, with its huge mouth, a belly that looks like a badly sagging neck, and long, curving, glassy teeth, made the cover of _Time_ magazine in 1995 as an example of a true sea monster. Its scientific group name says it all: _Melanocetus_, which means "black sea monster." The Atlantic wolffish's appearance isn't improved by its smile. It has four to six long fangs and several rows of teeth it uses to crush prey. It even has teeth in its throat. The frilled shark, named for a feathery arrangement of gills, isn't as dainty as its name suggests. Its 6-foot-7 (2 m) body is like an eel's, but its head resembles a rattlesnake's. Its long jaw enables it to open wide and swallow prey whole. It can hold prey tight with its 300 teeth.

SEA-MONSTER CULTURE

Other sea monsters have been reported by boaters, anglers, or even people out for Sunday drives. These reports have been investigated by sheriffs. They've been the subjects of news stories. Sea monsters have been the targets of researchers armed with sophisticated cameras and other underwater sensing devices. But they've never been captured. Photos of sea monsters tend to be blurry and confusing. For those very reasons, they continue to tantalize people.

The most well-known creature is probably the Loch Ness Monster. Loch Ness is in a narrow crevasse running across Scotland, known as the Great Glen **Fault**. The lake is 24 miles (38.6 km) long. It is only one mile (1.6 km) wide. But it reaches as deep as 745 feet (227 m). Fed by **peat**-filled streams, its water is brown and murky. A bomber that crash-landed in Loch Ness on a training flight in 1940 wasn't recovered until 1985.

In the sixth century A.D., an Irish missionary came across a long, slithery creature attacking a swimmer in Loch Ness. He ordered it to stop and chased it back into the water. Centuries went by before the creature was seen again. But after a road was built around the lake in the 1930s, sightings became more frequent. **Cryptozoologists**, researchers, and photographers probed the water, and "Nessie" became a global celebrity. Some determined it was a living dinosaur, trapped in the lake when its connections to the sea were pinched off millions of years ago. Some cryptozoologists say it's a *Basilosaurus*, a kind of whale with an alligator-like head that went extinct about 34 million years ago. But even organized searches, using dozens of boats and sophisticated electronics, have found little more than shadows.

Dozens of such monsters are said to live in other

bodies of water around the world. Many are described as horse-headed or serpent-like, showing little more of themselves than a line of trailing humps. "Chessie," a serpentine monster reportedly dwelling in Chesapeake Bay, has even become a popular symbol on government and environmental groups' websites. However, a manatee that wandered through the bay in the 1990s was also nicknamed Chessie.

Chessie, of course, rhymes with Nessie. It also rhymes with "South Bay Bessie," a creature sighted by sailors on Lake Erie as early as 1793. In 1998, a family spotted a disturbance in the water about 500 feet (152 m) off the lake's southern shore. Bubbles gave way to a long ripple, and then to three black humps, which appeared to be part of a moving, living creature. Or was it driftwood or a boat wake silhouetted by the setting sun? Or was it a **seiche** (*SAYSH*), common in Lake Erie?

People on two of Wisconsin's most popular recreational lakes, Geneva and Delavan, have seen monsters sticking their long necks above the water for more than a century. On the border between New York and Vermont, Lake Champlain has its own monster, "Champ." A picnicking family took its picture from close range in 1977. It appeared serpentine, about 24 to 78 feet (7.3–23.8 m) long. Was it a lake sturgeon or some ancient refugee? Was it a *Basilosaurus*? Could it have been a relative of Nessie's? No one's determined that—yet.

In British Columbia, Okanagan Lake is a bigger version of Loch Ness. It is 69 miles (111 km) long and 3 miles (4.8 km) wide. It's 750 feet (229 m) deep. Its best-known resident is Ogopogo, another serpentine monster spotted many times through the years. In 2004, a man on a houseboat, awakened by thumping in the night, took a video that showed a 15-foot-long

Even though Champ, the alleged sea monster of Lake Champlain, has never been proven to exist, it is protected by law in New York and Vermont.

(4.6 m), slimy, greenish beast with several humps at a distance of about 150 feet (45.7 m). The video didn't convince everybody there was a monster lurking. But in the early 1990s, Ogopogo was shown with a horse-shaped head and a forked tail on a Canadian postage stamp. Ogopogo has one characteristic other sea monsters do not: its name is the same spelled forward or backward.

Monuments to these creatures are common along the shores of the waters where they live. They are important tourist draws. Loch Ness attracts about one million visitors every year. Many want to get close to the mystery of Nessie or hope to catch a glimpse! They contribute about $32.3 million to the local **economy**. The Loch Ness Centre and Exhibition has offered programs on monster-related research for more than 30 years. Nessie still hasn't been caught or pictured, but people keep coming.

Some of the world's most famous sea monsters have never been seen and have never sparked the interest of researchers. That's because they're fictional creations. They've emerged from poems, books, and movies. Many scare people, anyway.

The American horror writer H. P. Lovecraft invented one such creature, called Cthulhu (*KLUL-hloo*). Cthulhu bore a strange resemblance to a giant squid, with long tentacles hanging from where a face should be. It also had wings and was hundreds of feet tall. Cthulhu makes frequent appearances in modern video and board games.

The shark in the 1975 movie *Jaws* made people jump out of their seats when it flung itself onto the boat of its pursuers. That shark was so terrifying that more than 50 movies with sharks as villains followed. Those films have enhanced the shark's fearsome image. In the 1999 film *Deep Blue Sea*, scientists enhance sharks' intelligence. The sharks become more vicious killers than they are in nature. The 2013 made-for-television movie *Sharknado* combined killer sharks with menacing weather in Los Angeles. Some naturalists think fear of sharks is a problem. They say it has made people think sharks should be destroyed. But most sharks represent no threat to humans. Humans kill an estimated 100 million sharks per year, whereas sharks attack about 50 people each year, killing only 6 to 10.

Melville's great white whale was hunted by the vengeful Captain Ahab. But the ship's entire crew went down with Ahab (except for the narrator). Whales were pictured as fierce fighters in the 19th century, the heyday of whaling. They were often shown biting boats in half and ramming ships. A 1977 movie, *Orca*, involved a vengeful killer whale (a dolphin species in ac-

H. P. Lovecraft created the Cthulhu for his 1928 short story "The Call of Cthulhu," in which people were driven insane simply by looking at the creature.

tuality). But in recent years, whales in films and stories have been portrayed as gentle, intelligent, and nurturing. That may be a reaction to the aggressive hunting that has dramatically reduced their numbers.

The giant squid in the 1954 Disney adaptation of *Twenty Thousand Leagues under the Sea* was frightful enough that the movie won that year's Academy Award for special effects. But another monster emerged that had even greater cultural impact: Godzilla. First appearing in a Japanese film, Godzilla looked a lot like a *Tyrannosaurus rex*. It was the first in a long line of gigantic, reptilian sea monsters that carries forward in popular culture. Today, such creatures might combine all manner of threatening features: flight, fire-breathing, speed, strength, and just plain old ugliness. And until we know more about the sea, people will continue to wonder what is really down there.

Cryptozoology Kings

Sea monsters regularly travel throughout science fiction. But they are also central to cryptozoology. Usually, cryptozoologists work to prove the existence of hidden or unseen creatures. The Loch Ness Monster is one of the best-known examples. Most scientists look down on cryptozoology for relying too much on mythology and folk tales. Bernard Heuvelmans, a Belgian-French scientist, is regarded as the father of cryptozoology. He held a **doctorate** in zoology. His first book, *On the Track of Unknown Animals*, sold one million copies. Heuvelmans's second book was *In the Wake of the Sea Serpents*. He was also a jazz musician. He died in 2001. Another key cryptozoologist is Loren Coleman (pictured). Coleman has written extensively about Bigfoot as well as lake monsters. His book with Patrick Huyghe, *The Field Guide to Lake Monsters, Sea Serpents, and Other Mystery Denizens of the Deep*, features a 14-point classification system for unknown sea and lake creatures. Coleman has been a consultant on numerous television shows and films and has written more than two dozen books. He founded the International Cryptozoology Museum in Portland, Maine.

GETTING TO THE BOTTOM OF IT

You would think that a shark that can grow to a length of 18 feet (5.5 m) and weighs more than one ton (0.9 t) would be familiar to sailors, swimmers, and scientists. You'd think there might even be some famous stories or books about it. But that is not the case with the megamouth shark. This type of shark had never been seen until one became entangled with the anchor of a U.S. Navy ship near Hawaii in 1976. Since then, only about 100 megamouths have been seen or caught.

That illustrates how much we still don't know about the seas and the creatures in them. Some scientists say our ancestors crawled out of the sea. But lately, humans have not been far below the surface. The world record for diving on a single breath, 831 feet (253 m), was set in 2012 by Austrian Herbert Nitsch. The scuba-diving depth record, 1,090 feet (332 m), was set by Egyptian Ahmed Gabr in 2014. Scuba diving deeper than 130 feet (39.6 m) is considered extremely risky because of the pressure of the water and the need to breathe gases other than oxygen. A naval submarine is believed to be able to drop safely to 1,600 feet (488 m).

That might seem to limit how much underwater exploring people can do. But technology has created some new options. Small and tough submersibles carry people and equipment far deeper than they were able to go in the past. *Alvin*, a submersible built in 1964, explored the wreck of the *Titanic* 12,500 feet (3,810 m) below the North Atlantic. It later dove to 14,800 feet (4,511 m). The Mariana Trench, between Japan and New Guinea, is the deepest part of all the world's oceans. It's about 36,070 feet (10,994 m) deep. (That's nearly a mile and a half [2.4 km] deeper than Mount Everest is high.) It's also protected by

Submersibles (opposite) enable people to reach the depths of the oceans, including such places as the Mariana Trench (illustrated below, in contrast with Mount Everest).

the U.S. as the Marianas Trench Marine National Monument. There have been four known descents to the bottom of the trench. The first was *Trieste*, owned by the U.S. Navy, in 1960. Two men were aboard. The next two crafts were unmanned. One was the Japanese *Kaiko* in 1995. The other was *Nereus* in 2009. (Owned and operated by the Woods Hole Oceanographic Institution in Massachusetts, *Nereus* was crushed and destroyed during a dive in the western Pacific Ocean in 2014.) The next manned descent was in 2012 in the *Deepsea Challenger*. It was piloted by *Titanic* film director James Cameron.

The National Oceanic and Atmospheric Administration (NOAA) is known for watching the air currents above us. But it also explores the

depths of the sea. Its *Okeanos Explorer* is a 224-foot (68.3 m) former navy ship converted in 2008 to conduct ocean research. The vessel has traveled the world. It maps the seafloor, tracks pollution, and investigates undersea eruptions. It also observes what kinds of animals are living down below. To do that, it carries electronic equipment such as **sonar** and remotely operated vehicles (ROVs). Researchers on the ship use computers to guide ROVs through the sea to investigate things and places people can't access. NOAA offers daily *Okeanos* updates on Facebook.

So what are researchers finding? In the Mariana Trench, they've found bacteria, sea cucumbers (animals that look like plants), and **amoeba**-like creatures called forams. Sea monsters may be born there, but they're more likely to grow and become recognizable in shallower water. That's where most sea life thrives, because it's warmer and there's more food. Luckily for researchers, it's also easier for humans to reach.

The ocean's middle depths are called the twilight zone. Also the name of a popular television show in the 1960s, that twilight zone was a place where people had strange and sometimes horrifying encounters and met strange creatures. The oceanic version has some similar features. It's the area from 600 to 3,300 feet (183–1,006 m) below the surface. Sunlight cannot penetrate deeper than 2,000 feet (610 m). No light means no plant life. It's cold—just 39 to 41 °F (3.9 to 5 °C). The pressure is nearly 100 times greater than it is at the surface, so it would crush a human being. But strange creatures like the giant squid live there. That's also where the coelacanth was rediscovered in 1938. Other alarming residents include poisonous pufferfish and cuttlefish. The cuttlefish, like giant squid and octopuses, can change its color in an instant to match its surroundings.

Living in near darkness, twilight zone creatures such as sea cucumbers display features that seem unnatural to those of us who enjoy sunlight.

The website of the *Okeanos Explorer* has an extensive collection of photos of creatures, corals, and other items its researchers have encountered. It's called the Benthic Deepwater Animal Identification Guide. Some sea-monster candidates can be found there.

In 2006 alone, 30 new species of fish were discovered off the coast of Borneo. And in 2016, a team of researchers from England's University of Southampton announced the discovery of six animal species deep in the Indian Ocean. Among their finds was a snowy-white crab known as a yeti crab. It was named after another rarely seen creature, the yeti, or Abominable Snowman. All the creatures were found in a mineral-rich area with many **hydrothermal vents**. That prompted researchers to note that the "new" animals might be vulnerable to mining in the near future.

In 2017, a team of researchers working in deep water off eastern Australia discovered hundreds of previously unknown species. They were searching down to 13,000 feet (3,962 m). One of their finds was the truly terrifying deepsea lizardfish. The pale-bodied, big-eyed fish, which can grow to be more than 2 feet (0.6 m) long, doesn't find much food at 1,969 to 11,483 feet (600–3,500 m) below the surface. It compensates by aggressively devouring anything it encounters, including other lizardfish, with its mouthful of impressively jagged and sharp teeth.

The team also rediscovered a "faceless" fish, which had not been seen for 144 years. The fish is gelatinous, like an eel, and lacks eyes. Its mouth is on the bottom of its body, and two nostrils are on top of the head.

Creatures without eyes might certainly fit the monster profile. Scientists digging around in caves in Croatia from 2014 to 2016 found a new species of cave salamander. Blind cave salamanders get around using smell

Bizarre-looking anglerfish use a rodlike appendage to attract prey as they wobble along near the seafloor.

43

and touch. Researchers also found a see-through snail.

Today's news media is delighted to report such finds. They show that there are indeed new things (and sometimes very old things) under the sun. Even so, we live in a skeptical age. Sea monsters? We know that the most famous picture of the Loch Ness Monster was a hoax—a toy serpent's body attached to a toy submarine. Will continuing discoveries of strange undersea creatures make us less willing to believe in sea monsters? You never know. The sea is still deep, dark, and mostly unexplored.

"If and when the first irrefutable water horse or classic sea serpent evidence finally turns up, any of the monster classifiers lucky enough to still be around will probably not care whether every detail of their categories match the actual creature," writes author Linda Godfrey. "They and every sea-monster witness through history will finally be vindicated."

In-Depth Studies The HMS *Challenger* was a former British Navy warship converted into the world's first oceanic research vessel. The 225-foot (68.6 m) **corvette** was stripped of all but two of its guns. It was equipped with laboratories, extra cabins, scientific equipment, a dredging deck, and 181 miles (291 km) of rope for pulling up samples from the ocean below. It left Portsmouth, England, in 1872 with a crew of 216, plus 21 officers and 6 scientists. For nearly 4 years, under both sail and steam, it circled the globe, covering 68,930 miles (110,932 km). It even traveled to Antarctica. Seafloor samples were collected, and scientists measured depths, temperatures, currents, and water chemistry. They discovered more than 4,700 plants and animals. Surprising to them, the samples did not resemble each area's fossils; instead they were "new." The report on the results took 23 years to complete and filled 29,500 pages in 50 volumes. The voyage is regarded as the birth of oceanography.

It is known for finding the deepest spot in the world's oceans. That area, located in the Mariana Trench, is known as Challenger Deep. The U.S. space shuttle *Challenger* was named for the ocean research vessel.

Field Notes

amoeba: jellylike, single-cell creatures that change shape and move and eat by extending a foot-like structure known as a pseudopod

corvette: a small, lightly armed but highly maneuverable warship

cryptozoologists: people who study reports and other evidence of animals unrecognized by most scientists

doctorate: the highest level of academic degree

economy: the wealth and resources of a place

fault: a crack in the earth's crust

hydrothermal vents: openings in the earth's surface from which heated water emerges

mythology: traditional stories, usually concerning the early history of a people or explaining a natural or social phenomenon

peat: brown, partially decayed plant material that can be dried and used for fuel

scuba: an acronym from "self-contained underwater breathing apparatus"; a type of diving that uses special equipment to be able to breathe under water

seiche: a swell of water pushed by wind from one end of a landlocked body of water to the other before flowing back

sonar: a technique using sound waves to navigate, find, or communicate with other objects under water

submersibles: vessels that can work deep under water, like submarines

terrain: a stretch of land and its physical features

Selected Bibliography

Ellis, Richard. *The Search for the Giant Squid*. New York: Lyons Press, 1998.

Godfrey, Linda S. *Lake and Sea Monsters*. New York: Chelsea House, 2008.

Hogenboom, Melissa. "Are Massive Squid Really the Sea Monsters of Legend?" BBC Earth. http://www.bbc.com/earth/story/20141212-quest-for-the-real-life-kraken.

Hoyt, Erich. *Creatures of the Deep: In Search of the Sea's "Monsters" and the World They Live In*. Buffalo, N.Y.: Firefly Books, 2001.

McKerley, Jennifer Guess. *The Kraken*. Detroit: KidHaven Press, 2008.

Miller, Karen. *Monsters and Water Beasts: Creatures of Fact or Fiction?* New York: Henry Holt, 2007.

Websites

AMERICAN MUSEUM OF NATURAL HISTORY: SEA MONSTERS
https://www.amnh.org/exhibitions/mythic-creatures/water-creatures-of-the-deep/sea-monsters/

NATIONAL OCEANIC AND ATMOSPHERIC ADMINISTRATION: OCEAN EXPLORER
http://oceanexplorer.noaa.gov/

Index